FUNDAMENTALS

OF GETTING

RICH

Understand the Maths and Systems that Make People Rich

KARTIK RATHORE

Made with ♥ on the Notion Press Platform

www.notionpress.com

Dedicated to all the Scientist, Inventors, and Innovators of the world.

Table of Contents

Introduction

This book is the result of enquiry into the questions like-

1. Why some people are richer than others?
2. If hard work is the key, why working-class people are not growing rich despite doing 10-12 hours of work every day?
3. How to get rich?
4. What are the things about money that rich knows but poor and middle class does not?
5. What system is working for the rich that makes them richer?

I tried to look for the answers of these questions, and I found the answers in most fundamental science, that is, mathematics.

There is a clear mathematics, which I have called as income equation, which determines who will end up being rich, and who will end up poor and middle class?

After all, wealth is quantifiable, which means you can represent wealth by a number. If it's a number, all the rules of mathematics apply on this number.

And yes, I am not talking about compounding. Nowadays most people know about compounding.

I have discussed fundamental mathematics and reasons which are not commonly known and not much discussed.

This book mathematically proves how a salaried job keeps a person in middle class. By simple math, I have also explained why entrepreneurship is the way if you want to get rich.

In this book, I have introduced the concept of proportional and disproportional sources of income. This knowledge about wealthy is so fundamental that it should be taught in schools.

Apart from that, I have also explained why and how YouTubers and Instagram influencers are making way more money than well educated professionals?

The goal of the book is to find a way to get rich, which was followed by many billionaires like Elon musk and Mark Zuckerberg.

Later, in the book, I have explained what kind of education you should get to become rich?

The book ends with a chapter on how a country can grow rich?

After reading this book, in order to become rich, you will have to work hard, but you will have better idea on what things you should work hard.

Best wishes,
Kartik

Chapter 1

How A Job Keeps You Middle Class?

Being employed in someone else's organisation has its own advantages. Surety of getting a monthly income, keeps stress and anxiety low. Also, a salaried employee in country like India is comparatively well off than majority of the population, which includes farmers and unskilled labourers. And there is no denial that highly skilled employees like software engineers, managers etc. earn high salary and occupy their place in the middle class or upper middle class of India.

But when it comes to getting rich, like super Rich, job also comes with certain disadvantages. And these disadvantages are the reasons why people who work 10-12 hours a day for an organisation or individual still get stuck in middle class trap.

Many people say this, but in this chapter, we will look mathematically, why is this so?

Before we get to these disadvantages, we need to understand how it is decided that how much money is to be paid to an employee?

I have designed an equation which I have called as income equation. This Income Equation tries to answer this question.

Income (salary) of an employee = f(Expertise, Time)

Salary ∝ Expertise (Skill)
Salary ∝ Time

To put in simpler words, the income (salary) of an employee depends on his expertise (what can he do?) and the amount of time he works.

Better skilled a person is, more will be his salary. For example, any engineer will be paid more than an unskilled labourer. A doctor is paid more than a nurse. This is general knowledge. Which you might have already observed around you.

Second is time, the greater number of hours, you work, more will be the salary. this holds true in both cases. The salary of the day depends on the number of hours worked in a day and salary of the month or year also depends on the number of days worked in a month or year.

Coming back to our original question, the disadvantages of the jobs, that stops a person from getting rich. Since the salary of the person depends on his or her expertise and time, so let us try to understand the problem of getting paid for your expertise and time.

Problems of getting paid for your time

Problems of getting paid for your time are equally applied to both, the salaried employees, and the self-employed professionals.

By self employed professionals. I mean people who do not work under somebody else's organisation or individuals. For example, doctors having their own clinic and lawyers practising independently.

We will understand the problems of getting paid for your time by taking the example of a self-employed doctor. However same mathematics of income also applies to a salaried class person.

He's a good doctor and charges 100 rupees fees from one patient, if he treats 10 patients in a hour.

He is making 1000 rupees per hour.
(₹100*10 = ₹1000).
Assuming he works for 8 to 10 hours a day, then he makes approximately ₹8000-₹10,000 a day.

Which is a huge amount, and he might be earning more than 98-99% people on the earth.

Now this doctor wants to increase his income by doing the hard work, he works 2 to 4 hours extra and earns ₹2000 to ₹4000 extra.
Well and good.

What if he tries to increase his income even further. Is it possible?

Practically speaking, on an average a normal person cannot work more than 14 hours a day every day.

Assume he is a superhuman and he works 18 hours a day, or 20 hours a day.

Can he stretch beyond that?

The answer is No!!!!

That is the biggest disadvantage of getting paid for our time.

THE TIME IN A DAY IS LIMITED.

THE NUMBER OF HOURS IN A DAY ARE LIMITED.

So, number of hours that our doctor can work in a day is limited. Fixed. It has a maximum value i.e. 24hours. There is no way a day can have more than 24 hours.

Since maximum time in a day is limited, so maximum output a salaried employee or individual professional can generate in a day is LIMITED.

And since income of our doctor depends on number of hours he works, no. of patients he treats, so naturally maximum amount he earns in a day will also be LIMITED.

This is the biggest disadvantage of getting paid for our time. And this is not just limited to the doctors. This applies to all the salaried employees and professionals like teachers, lawyers, CAs, etc.

This is what I call **Proportionate sources of income**, where income is directly proportional to no. of hours the individual has worked.

There are also **Disproportionate sources of income**, where the money you earn does not depend on no. of hours you worked and limitation of having 24 hours in a day does not affect the maximum amount that can be earned in day. That is how The Rich People earn. About which I have discussed in Chapter 5(The disproportionate Income sources).

No doubt, a doctor earning ₹8000 to ₹10,000 per day for is a huge amount, he can live a very comfortable life with this money. And it is a noble profession. They have all my respect.

But since we are trying to understand what makes the rich, the rich? I want to highlight the limitation and ceiling we have on the maximum amount that can be earned if our income depends on number of hours we work.

So, if your income depends on the number of hours, you work; be cautious. You have a ceiling on the maximum amount you can earn in a day. And that will make it even harder for you to become rich.

We took the example of doctor, but they are one of the highest paid professionals. Take the case of unskilled labours who earn as little as ₹200 to ₹300 per day. Now you can imagine why they remain poor despite doing all the hard physical work every day.

There are also disadvantages of getting paid for your expertise and skill if you are working in someone else's company, but we will discuss about that later.

There are few more disadvantages of being an employee in an organisation which I will discuss in later chapters.

Summary

- Income of a salaried employee and independent professionals depends on number of hours they work.
- Since the number of hours in a day are limited, the maximum amount, these people can earn in a day is limited. So, no matter how hard they work they cannot earn beyond a limit.

Chapter 2

The Income Equation of The Rich

In the previous chapter, we discussed the income equation of salaried employees and individual professionals and how their maximum output and salary had an upper limit.

Now we will analyse and see why business owners don't have these disadvantages? And how do they overcome the limitation of time in a day?

For that we need to understand how businessmen earn the money?

We all earn money by selling something. And to produce some output we need some inputs. A salaried employee or individual professional sells his service. And to produce that service he/she needs time as an input.

Now analyse this for a business owner. A business owner sells the goods and services that his company produces.

A businessman needs land (place to do work), labour(people) and capital (money, machinery) to establish a factory or office. With these things, he makes a product or service and sales into the market.

Thus, the income equation for a business owner is very much different from a salaried employee.

For a business owner –

Income (Profit) = (Price of Output)- (Cost of Inputs)

Output is the final product that he sells and inputs are land, labour, and capital.

So,
Income of a business owner = (Price of final product) - (Cost of Land, Labour & Capital)

Now let's discuss the advantages of this income equation.

As we had discussed in the case of salaried employees and individual professionals that there was limitation and upper ceiling on maximum income because of limited hours in a day. Now, let's examine, do the business owners also have such limitations and ceilings?

Let us start with input side (land, labour & capital)

1.Land- or I should use the word "Place to do work". A Business owner needs a place to establish a factory or office. The advantages here is that we have lots and lots of land available to establish factories and do the work. Even if you don't own land, you can always take an office or a piece of land on rent. So practically there is no limitation on availability of land.

2.Labour -With so many unemployed youths in countries like India, there is no lack of availability of labours. Sometimes there may not be availability of skilled labours, but you can always skill the people or pay higher salaries and people will be available to do the work. So, here also we are seeing that we have huge supply of labours, and they are also available on monthly rent, called salary. (I am being bit harsh here but yeah!). A businessman also has 24 hours in a day but since there are people working for him in his organisation, he overcomes the limitation of time by employing more people in his company and getting more things done in the same 24 hours. This is how disadvantage of having limited time is overcome.

3.**Capital**- Third thing that a business owner needs is capital, that is basically money to buy machinery and raw material. Even if a business owner doesn't have money of his own, business loan is available at rent (called interest) . There is enough availability of capital in the banks. After all, they keep calling you for taking loans. Practically speaking, you might have some problems in getting the loan but if you have good credit history and/or some collateral, then you should not get any problem in getting the loan. Banks might not give you loans more than an amount but as your company grows bigger the amount of loan that you can get from banks also grows. Also, there are other channels to get the funding like investors, venture capitalist, and government funds. If your ideas are good enough, people are ready to invest and waiting with their money.

So as far as input side is concerned, what we are seeing is that whatever a business owner needs (land, labour, and capital), are available in unlimited supply. But to be more accurate let's say all these 3 things are available in huge supply. And interestingly all three (land, labour and capital) are available on rent.

-

Now let's look at the output side of the business and try to find if there is any limitation.

Yes, there is one limitation.

That is market size.

The no. of buyers for a product are not infinite. Every product has a market size. That is the maximum number of units that can be sold or demanded.

But interestingly, this limitation can be overcome (to certain extent).

Here are some ways to overcome this limitation –

1.When market in a country or a region is saturating, companies can start exploring new markets in foreign countries and start exporting their products.
2. Companies can launch multiple products. Example- smartphone manufacturers have entered in accessory market, some even started to manufacture tablets and laptops.
3. Once company has earned money by one business, and if there is not much possibility of growing in that particular business, then they can start new business in some other sectors. Reliance is a great example.

So, market size for a particular product may be limited but overall market size is not limited. Some or other products are always in demand. Something or other can always be sold and overall possibility to sell is not limited.

So, what we are seeing is the income of a businessman does not depend on amount of time he himself has worked. His income depends on cost and availability of land, labour, capital, and market size. Land, labour and capital are available in huge supply and there is always a market for some products. And there is huge possibility to grow.

This unlimited supply of land, labour and capital creates possibility for business owners to keep growing and keep increasing their income.

Let me explain my point with an example of a businessman who manufacturers smartphones.

He has a factory where he manufactures his smartphones. He has a labour force and machinery to manufacture a maximum of 1000 units/month. And he also sells the same number of smartphones every month. He makes a profit of ₹1000 on every smartphone that he sells. Which means his monthly income is ₹1000 x 1000= ₹10 lakh.

Now he works on the quality of the product, introduces some new features, spend some money in marketing and introduces a new version of the smartphones.

People liked it and his 1000 units are sold out in 15 days. Next month, he is expecting to sell more than 1000 units, but his company's manufacturing capacity is maximum of 1000 units/month.

Now what will you do?

He will go to the bank/investors. He will show his numbers. He will discuss about the growth in sales and his expected sales in upcoming months and ask for a loan.

Obviously, Banks/investors will be impressed. They will give him the loan/funding. With this money, he will take on rent a manufacturing facility (Land), he hires few more people (Labour) buy some machinery and raw material and spend some money in marketing.

Three months later, he successfully sales 2000 units per month. Now let's calculate his monthly income ₹1000 x 2000= ₹ 20 lakh.

He just doubled his income.

Obviously, these are hypothetical numbers but the point I wanted to highlight was that there is huge possibility for growth in business.

In order to double his salary, the doctor had to double his working hours, but in order to double the salary, did the businessman also had to double his working hours?

Not really.
He can hire an able manager to handle the other factory.

Now look at the case of salaried employees and Independent Professionals-

As we had seen in the previous chapter for a salaried employee and individual professionals, there was no room for growth of income because of limited number of hours in a day.

The only way, a salaried employee's income increases is if his employer decides. An employee gets happy if he gets a salary hike of 20 to 25% yearly. In organised sector in India, salaries are revised on annual basis, which means a salaried employee has to wait for a year to have a growth of 20-25% in his salary. Sometimes there is no year-on-year increment as well.

For professionals like doctors and lawyers, if they want to increase their income, apart from working more hours they might increase their fees, but again
(a) you cannot increase your fees drastically.
(b) you cannot keep increasing your fees every now and then. Once you increase your fees you wait for next one or two year to revise your fees.

But switching companies and increasing consultation fees does not take away the disadvantage of "limited time of the day" and upper ceiling of the income.

Businesses can be SCALED.
Jobs cannot be SCALED.
And **SCALING is a Superpower.**

Scaling means to make things bigger, to enlarge a system to generate more output.

Our smartphone manufacturer can invest his profit in the business, take some more loan or find an investor, hire some more people and buy some more machinery and can grow his sells to 10,000 units, 20,000 units and even beyond that. As long as there is demand in the market, he has the room to grow and as he keeps growing his income keeps increasing.

This is how the unlimited supply of land, labour and capital helps business owners to keep increasing their income.

That's the superpower of SCALE that businesses owners enjoy, and that's not the advantage salaried employees and individual professionals have.

Apart from this, there are certain tax benefits that business owners enjoy, and salaried employees do not. But I do not want to get into that you can find those details on the Internet.

I do acknowledge the challenges of a business owner, and I also do know that businesses do fail. But my main goal was to highlight the mathematics that makes the rich, the rich and keep the salaried employees, middle class or poor.

Salaried employees and individual professionals might be experts in their field, but business owners hire the experts on rent (Salary).

This mathematics was never told to us, (at least majority of us). And that's Why a lot of Indians are engaged in being an expensive labour. Majority of us do all the expensive college courses to get a good job in a company that pays well.

Does that mean I am advocating not to go to college? Or not to become an expert?

No, definitely not. I have explained my point in detail in chapter number 7(Education to get Rich) where I explain what kind of education you should get and what kind of expert should you become if you want to become rich.

As done in this chapter. I will put more logical and mathematical arguments, that will further explain why entrepreneurship is the way if you want to become rich.

That's why unlike salaried employees and individual professionals; the income of businessmen is not limited. There is always possibility to earn more.

Summary

✦To earn, we need to sell something. A salaried employee and individual professional need time (as an input) to produce output, and since maximum time in a day is limited, their maximum output is also limited, and so does their salaries.

✦ A Business owner need Land, Labour and Capital to generate output, and all of these 3 things are available in huge supply and that's why he/she can produce as much output is being demanded by the market.

✦ Because of this unlimited supply of Land, Labour and Capital, Business Owners can SCALE their businesses to produce more output.

✦ With growing output and sells, the income of business owner also keeps increasing and thus for a business owner virtually there is no upper limit of money that can be earned in a day.

Chapter 3

How Do People Get Rich?

Since we are trying to understand the fundamentals of getting rich, let's ask a fundamental question, what does being rich mean?

As we all know, to be rich means to have a lot of money, a lot of assets.

As of 8 November 2024, Mukesh Ambani's net worth is US$90 billion. That is equal to ₹7,50,000 crore. Our mind doesn't comprehend numbers very well. Let me give you another perspective. ₹7,50,000 crore is such a big amount that if you fill 12*12*12 feet^3 room with ₹500 denomination notes, then approximately 50,000 room will be filled. (Ask ChatGPT)

By now, as we understand that if Mukesh Ambani had been a salaried employee or individual professional, he would not have earned even 0.00001% of his total net worth.

Which gives rise to question how do people get this much rich?

It does not work like; RBI prints all the money and supply it to him.

What actually happens is money flows from masses to some people who eventually get richer.

Which gives rise to few more fundamental questions-

1.How does and why does the money flow towards some people?

2.How does and why does money flow from one person to another?

3.And Why world pays you (or anybody else for that matter)?

And in later chapters, we will also see how this money can flow towards you.

So, let's try to understand.

We are a market economy and in a market economy, we exchange money in return of some goods or service that we sell or buy.

For example, somebody needs biscuit. If I give him, he will give me money in return.
If I need a shirt, I will go to store. I give them the money. They will give me shirt. Simple. As you already understand all of this.

Here, I would like to also give a description about "Services". On a daily basis we buy and use a lot of goods, for example - car, bike, electronics, food items, furniture, clothes etc. These are the things that we can touch and feel. And when we buy them, we pay some money.

Apart from buying goods, we also pay money to some professionals for their service. For example, a barber who cuts our hairs. He does not give us goods, but he helps us in some way and that's why we pay him. Similarly, a doctor treats us, a teacher teaches, lawyer gives legal consultation. All these people do not give any physical goods to us, but they help us in some way, that help is called "service".

So basically, in a market economy, we either sell goods or service. Goods are physical things that you can touch. Services are intangible help that you get from the professionals.

Similarly, Mukesh Ambani gives us data, petrol, diesel, gas, footwear, electronics, groceries etc. and in return we give him money.

So basically, everybody who is earning any money in the economy, is a seller of something. Even a salaried employee is also the seller of his service to a company or an individual. The company or individual needed some people to finish some tasks. These people (salaried employees) finish those tasks and solve the problem for the company or the individual. In return that company or individual gives them the money(salary).

If that's clear to you, let's move forward.

Another basic thing which you might know is that these goods or services are sold at a price which is more than their input cost. (generally speaking).

This difference of selling price of the goods and input cost is the profit margin.
So basically,

Profit = Selling Price - Input Cost

This is the income of the company or the individual when that good or service is sold.

Which is easy to understand.

But this profit is realised only if those goods and services are sold.

Which gives rise to a question, why would anybody buy my product?

And the answer is, if that product or service solves some of their problems or it makes them happier or it makes their life easier or fulfil some need. It's all one and the same thing, basically decrease pain and increase pleasure.

Think of all the purchases that you made recently, all of them were intended for this, either decrease pain and/or increase pleasure, basically solve some problem.
You want to talk to a distant friend you have mobile phone, you are feeling cold you have a sweater, you want to save yourself from rain, there is umbrella. you want to watch Netflix, you have 5G Internet. you want to travel to a distant place you have a car. You got sick, you have a doctor to treat you. All these things, mobile phone, sweater, umbrella, the 5G Internet connection, car etc. Solve some of our problems and that's why we buy them.

Professionals like doctors, lawyers, architect, teachers, also solves some of our problems and in return we pay them.

So, market is a place where we solve each other's problem and in return we exchange money.

So, in the economy, everybody is solving some problems of others. If you are unemployed and you want to earn some money, solve some problems of somebody and he will give you the money.

Now a question arises, if everybody is solving some kind of the problem, then why is there so much income disparity? How, and why is somebody earning more than the others?

The difference is of **SCALE** and **MARGIN**.

Let's go through them one by one in detail.

The Scale

We discussed about scale in our previous chapter in terms of enlarging our business. Here we are discussing about scale in terms of <u>number of people whose problem we are solving.</u>

Assume that I am a business owner, and I made a product that solves a particular problem and on sale of one product, I make a profit of ₹10. And if I sell it to 100 people, my profit is ₹1000.
And if I sell it to 200 people, my profit is ₹2000.
Easy calculation.

More the no. of people whose problem I solve, more will be my reward (income).

So,
my income (profit) ∝ number of customers [Number of people whose problem my product or service solves]

An independent lawyer solves problem of 10 to 20 clients in a day, he gets money proportional to that number. and Since Mukesh Ambani sales data to 50 crore people in a day and thus makes money proportional to this number.

That's Scale.

The number of people whose problem you can solve, is the number of your customers.

The no. of people facing a problem is the potential customer base for the product that can solve that problem.

Apple, Amazon, Coca-Cola, Facebook, Google, Samsung, Reliance, Tata, Nestlé are companies that earn billions of dollars because they sell(serve) to millions and billions of people.

Compounding has got the appreciation it deserves, but as far as Scale is concerned, its strength and value are not as mainstream as of compounding.
But anyways,

"Scale is a Superpower"

More customers, More Income.

As we have already seen because of the limitation of number of hours in a day, the individual professional can serve a limited number of people only, and thus they have a limited income.

Let's discuss a little more about salaried employees.

As we had already discussed earlier in the chapter that everybody in the economy is a seller and so is a salaried employee.

Tell me, what is the number of customers for a salaried employee?

Unfortunately, only One.

Yeah, that's the thing. Indirectly it might look that a salaried employee is solving problem for more than one people, he is selling his services to many people. But technically, if you see the number of his customer is only one, that is, his employer.

It will be clearer with an example.
Take for example, A teacher (a salaried employee) working in a school owned by somebody else. The teacher might think I'm solving the problem for these many students, I am selling my service to these many students. But if you look closely that's not the case.

Since the owner cannot be physically present in every classroom, he must hire some people. So technically the teacher is solving the problem for the owner of school. The teacher is selling his services to the owner, who sells it forward to the students. So, the owner of the school is the reseller. The number of customers for teacher is only one. Students are the customers of the owner here.

If the no. of students increases then the profit of the owner will also increase, but it's highly likely that the teacher's salary may not increase, apart from yearly increment that he is supposed to get.

I do acknowledge that the employer is a big buyer of the service for a salaried employee and buys his services every day. But in an economy where your income depends on the number of customers you have. The major disadvantage for salaried employees is that they cannot increase the no. of customers. By moonlighting (working part time, after the main job) they can increase the no. of customers to two or three, but not beyond that.

Some people who do this part time jobs like driving uber or delivering food after their 9-5 jobs, do not realise that in such part time jobs their income once again depends on number of hours they work.

Which keeps their income limited and year on year they do not see as much growth in their incomes and as a result they are stuck in middle income trap.

Well, there is a way to overcome this limitation of having 24 hours in a day, and that is by **keep getting recurring income by working once.**

How does that work? That I have explained in upcoming chapters.

We consider a salary of ₹1,00,00 per month as a benchmark in India.
"Oh My God, he has a of salary ₹1,00,00 per month"
But If I ask you what you need to earn ₹1,00,000 per month?
There can be many permutations and combinations but here I have given two.
In order to earn ₹1,00,000, either you need 100 customers from whom you can have a profit of ₹1000 ***in whole month.*** (100*₹1000=₹100,000)
OR
You need 1000 customers from whom you can have a profit of ₹100 in whole month. (1000*₹100=₹1,00,000)

So, first highlight of this chapter is – To earn more money, solve the problems of as many people as you can. Larger the number of people whose problem you solve, larger is your customer base and more will be the amount of money you make.

Now let's discuss about the second thing

The Margin.

The importance of having a higher margin is easy to understand.

Having a higher margin per customer overall increases your profit.

If I have a customer base of 50 people, and if I get ₹100 margin from every customer. My income is 50*₹100= ₹5000.
If somehow, I increase my margin to ₹200 per customer, my income becomes 50*₹200= ₹10,000.

The idea is simple, more margin per customer you have, more will be your income.

By Profit Margin I mean **Net Profit Margin**, the profit, a company makes after deducting the depreciation, transportation, marketing, taxes, and all other expenditure.

Microsoft has approximately 35% as profit margin, NVIDIA has more than 55%. Some software companies, luxury goods companies and technology companies have more than 70% as their profit margins.

Which gives rise to question –
How can you get higher margins?

This is an important question, and I have discussed this in detail in next chapter.

Summary

✦In this chapter, we tried to find an answer to the question "Why some people earn more money than the others?"

✦ We discussed that to earn money, you have to sell something; and to sell something, your goods and services should solve some of the problems of the consumers. That means to decrease their pain and/or increase their pleasure.

✦ Larger the number of people whose problem you solve, larger will be your customer base and more amount of money you will make.

✦ This was the first part of the answer, The Scale part. We will explore the second part "How to get higher margins?" in next Chapter

Chapter 4

Innovate And Grow Rich

How to have Higher Profit Margins?

As we discussed Profit Margin is simply the difference between Price at which Output i.e. Goods/Services are sold and the Cost of Inputs.

Profit Margin = (Price of Output)- (Cost of Inputs)

So, if we are interested to increase the profit margins, then this can be done in two ways-
(i) **Maximise the selling cost of output** (product or service that we sell)
(ii)**Minimise the cost of inputs** (Raw material, Production cost, Marketing, etc)

Simple.

So, our task is to find out how can we cut the cost of inputs and sell our products at maximum possible price at which people still buy it?

Before giving the answer, if I ask you this question, "How can we cut input cost and maximise the price

of output?" Then more than 10 things will pop up in your head.
But if I have to give one umbrella word for everything that we can do then that word has to be **INNOVATION**.

And when I say innovation, I mean, innovation in every possible area that is involved, from making the product for the first ever time to final delivery at the consumer's home.

Innovation makes things more efficient and overall helps both the entrepreneur and consumers. We will understand in detail how Innovation is the key to higher profits and overall business success?
But let's first understand, what are the areas where a business can innovate?

So here are some steps/areas/aspects where businesses can innovate -

1. Innovation in Product/Service
2. Innovation in Business Model
3. Innovation in Process
4. Innovation in Marketing and Brand Building
5. Innovation in Customer Experience

There can be even more areas where entrepreneurs can innovate, but here I have taken the areas where innovation creates high to medium impact on the business.

In fact, an entrepreneur should keep looking for any inefficiencies in the system and improve it by innovative ideas at every possible stage to make things more efficient.

Now we will look at this innovations, one by one in detail. What is it? How it affects the businesses? What companies have done that particular type of innovation? How did they do it? How did it help them? and many more such things. Let's start.

INNOVATION IN PRODUCT/SERVICES

What is innovation in product and service?

The aim of any product or service is to solve some kind of problem. And when a person comes across a new problem, which has not been sold yet or the existing solutions are not efficient enough, then in such a scenario if this person makes a new product or service that solve this problem or increases the efficiency, then this can be called as an innovation at product/service level.

For example, back in the day, we had small feature phones with limited functionality. Smartphones are huge upgrade and great example of innovation. They can do a lot of things for us and help us in many ways.

Creation of new and innovative products often involves cutting edge technologies that completely disrupt the industry.

If it's completely a new product that has been made for the first time, then it is called invention. For example, the satellite internet by Starlink, self-driving cars by Tesla, etc. For this book, I have included the term "invention" in the "innovation" itself.

Out of all the areas in business, where innovation can be done, **innovating at product or service level, creates the maximum impact.** All other things are secondary. Product is the heart and soul of any business. If the product is not great, no amount of marketing works, but if the product is great even the word of mouth does the job.

So how does innovation increase the margin/profitability?

Well, the first thing is that innovation **cuts the cost.** New technologies are much more efficient than the old ones and thus saves the cost of making. Ex- **Reusability of Rockets**: SpaceX revolutionised the aerospace industry by developing reusable rockets, such as the Falcon 9. Traditionally, rockets were single-use, making space launches extremely expensive. By landing and reusing rocket boosters, SpaceX drastically reduced the cost of space launches.

Second, **innovation adds a lot of value.**

Innovation helps us to transform low value, raw material into high value finished products.

For example, sand may not be of high value, but once the same sand is transformed into semiconductor chips, it becomes highly valuable.

Third, **innovation increases the perceived value** of the product.

What is perceived value of the product?

Any product or service does not have an absolute fixed price. Their Price depends on how valuable we humans think that particular product/service is.
A glass of water at your home may not be of high price, its price is ₹15 in train, its price is ₹70 in cinema hall and the same water can be of any price in middle of the desert.

Perceived value is the worth or value A customer believes a product or service has, based on his subjective judgement. In monetary terms, perceive value of a product for consumer can be said as the maximum price, he/she is ready to pay for the product, based on his evaluation of its benefits, quality, and desirability.

Innovative products have higher perceived value. Because when there was no solution available for a problem and when the solution is introduced for the first time, we have a great opportunity to make profit. When innovative product is introduced in market; something that people has never seen before, then people are mesmerised by it, people now have what they always wanted. People want that novelty and are ready to pay a higher price, even if the cost of production for the company is not that high. Which ultimately results in higher margin.

For example, few years ago, when Apple was making disruptive innovation in iPhone, people used to lineup in huge numbers in front of Apple store to get the latest iPhone.

Innovations help us to create products which are durable and reliable and perform better. This perception of longer life increases the perceived value.

There is another reason why innovative products deliver higher margins. Unethical it might sound, but when high level of processing is done on raw material and with help of technology, and if the raw material is transformed into a finished product, then it is not possible for an average consumer to guess the input price, and thus consumers end up perceiving higher value and thus pay way higher than the input cost, which results in higher margin for the company.

For example, high-end smartphones and tablets are launched at ₹70,000-₹80,000 per piece. Then after 2-3 years, you can buy them for as low as ₹40,000. Even at ₹40,000 the company is definitely selling this product at fairly good enough profit margin. Which simply means that the input cost is even lower for the company, but the customer who made the purchase at ₹80,000 perceived its worth as ₹80,000 or more at that time and that's why they made the purchase.

What made the customer perceive the value of the smart phone so high?

Definitely the ignorance of consumers about the input cost is one factor but the innovation (the latest technology, stand out features etc.) that company has introduced in those smart phones made the consumer to perceive their value to higher level.

This way companies with the help of continuous innovation make products whose perceived value is way higher than their input costs and thus make high margins.

Which is not possible for low innovation, low technology products.

Take for example, wheat flour, which is a common commodity, and most of the people know how it is manufactured and what is it's cost. There is nothing much new that can be done with it. Which means, the perceived value of wheat flour is not very much higher than the input costs of production. That's why very high margin cannot be earned in this business.

In India, we pay ₹80 for a 45ml mosquito repellent refill. We think that it contains some amazing liquid. And that's why we perceive its value to be ₹80.
If you actually read the ingredients, 96.4% of it is just kerosene, 1% is perfume and 1 to 2% is the actual repellent Chemical.
I have done all the maths; it takes maximum of ₹10 to ₹15 to make one refill.

Same goes for perfume industry, hardly anybody knows how much it costs to the manufacturer.
If it smells good. It must be expensive.

Fourth, **Innovation and Innovation alone can create unique products.**

Innovation creates INTELLECTUAL PROPERTY (IP) for the company.

Intellectual property (IP) refers to the legal rights granted to person or companies over the creations of their minds. These rights give the creators exclusive control over the use, distribution, and commercialisation of their creations for a certain period.

Intellectual property is anything which is your original creation. In most cases, it's innovated or invented. It can be in the form of patents, copyrights, trademarks, trade secrets, designs etc.

For electronics product, it's circuit diagram can be called IP, for a software it's code, for a soap company, the chemical formula, for a car company it can be car's design, for a writer, his poems etc. can be called as it's IP.

Advantages IP gives is that once you have patent, copyright, trade secrets etc. for a product, others cannot use it. They must invent things for their own. Either they will not be able to invent it, or it will take some time for them. And that's why there is low competition in high tech product industries.

The price of commodities in economy is decided by demand and supply. If you successfully make a unique product, you can be the sole supplier of the product and you can create a monopoly. Even if you don't become a monopoly, inventions and innovations help you make products that are the best in their category. In such a case, you can definitely put a higher price tag on your products.

For example, the Google search engine, which itself is an innovative product and over the year, they have kept the innovation going, which puts them ahead of everybody else.

Apart from increasing margins, there are some **other benefits of Innovation: -**

1. If there does not exist a solution for a problem and if we can successfully make it then it becomes easier to get entry into the market. Sometimes inventions create a market for themselves. It becomes easier to get started. Moreover, the company picks the pace faster. For example – ChatGPT, A technologically advanced innovative product that does a lot of things, picked overnight. Another great example is Zerodha. Which made stock trading easier and is a bootstrapped profitable company.
2. Technology or IP that you have also becomes a barrier to entry for other market players. Take for example, if I think to start a laptop company tomorrow. All of a sudden, I cannot. From chip to circuit to assembly, it will take me a lot of time to figure out. But if I think of starting a Bhujiya(Namkeen, Sev) company, I can pick a Halwai from the street, raw material from market and start overnight. And that's the reason we have very few companies that make laptop and a lot of namkeen companies.
3. Continuous innovation also helps you to sustain in the market. Companies that did not innovate are replaced by the companies that did. Nokia, Blackberry, Kodak refused to upgrade and are now out of market.
4. Innovation also helps you in destroying monopolies or Duopolies. For a long time, hand wash market in India was dominated by two companies they sold their hand wash refill for ₹60 to

₹80. Godrej came up with ₹15 powder hand wash refill and everybody fallen in line.

That's the power of innovation.

Innovation as The Best Bet to Richness

Let me tell you a story.
This story is of an Indian entrepreneur Karsanbhai Patel, the founder of Nirma, who revolutionised the detergent market in India with an affordable product.

Karsanbhai Patel was born in 1945 in Ruppur, Gujarat, into a modest farming family.
He studied chemistry and started his career as a lab technician in a government department. While working, Karsanbhai observed that detergents available in the market were expensive and unaffordable for middle-class and lower-income families.
He developed a low-cost detergent powder in his backyard using his chemistry knowledge. The detergent was named "Nirma".
Patel sold his detergent door-to-door on his bicycle at ₹3 per kg, compared to the ₹13 charged by established brands like Surf.
The product quickly gained popularity due to its affordability and decent quality.

Word-of-mouth marketing and catchy jingles like "Sabki Pasand Nirma" helped in establishing the brand.
Patel faced tough competition from multinational companies like Hindustan Unilever. Despite having limited resources, he focused on cost efficiency, mass production, and a wide distribution network.
By the 1980s, Nirma became a household name, overtaking Surf as the market leader in India.
Later Karsanbhai diversified into products like soaps, toothpaste, and cosmetics.

Dr. Karsanbhai Patel demonstrated how knowledge of science, technology, and engineering can lead to innovation and business success. Karsanbhai's ability to solve a common problem with a simple yet innovative product led to the creation of a successful business and immense personal wealth.

You will see the same pattern in success stories of many entrepreneurs. They saw a problem. They used their knowledge to create an innovative solution and on the basis of that solution, they successfully created a business. Be it Mark Zuckerberg, Elon musk, Narayana Murthy, Jeff Bezos and many more.

We will always have some problems to solve. If we use technology to create innovative products, these innovative products can become foundation for a successful business.

Even if we cannot make a completely new product, there is always an eternal problem of inefficiency. Existing products can always be made more efficient and in lesser price. We can always choose this path. Just as Godrej helped in bringing the price of handwash refilled down significantly. Such innovations can be made in other fields as well, and a lot of new businesses can be created which will eventually pave the way for prosperity.

That was all I had to say about Innovation in Product and Service.

Now let's move to other innovations.

As I said earlier, innovation in product and service is the most important, and we also discussed why it's most important. But there are so many businesses who have products just as good as their competitors or sometime, even inferior product, but because of innovation in some other areas, they became successful.

Now let's move towards our second area of innovation, which is: -

INNOVATION IN BUSINESS MODEL

Business model innovation refers to the strategic redesign or creation of a company's framework for delivering value, generating revenue, and managing costs.

Unlike product/service innovation, which focus on product only, business model innovation changes the way a company operates, monetizes its offerings, or interacts with stakeholders. It involves rethinking how value is created, delivered, and captured to gain a competitive edge or meet emerging market demands.

In simple terms, a business model is the strategy by which you can generate more revenue by same products. It's about finding new ways to do business—whether by altering pricing models, introducing new revenue streams, or creating innovative customer engagement strategies.

Here Are Some Innovative Business Models that have been greatly successful: -

1. **Subscription Models**
Customers pay a recurring fee to access products or services.
Example: Netflix's subscription for streaming content.
Advantage: Predictable revenue and stronger customer relationships.

2. **Freemium Models**
Basic offerings are free, but advanced features are paid.
Example: Spotify's free version with ads and premium ad-free subscription.
Advantage: Attracts a large user base with minimal cost, converting some to paying customers.

3. **Bundling**
Combining multiple products or services into a single package at a discounted price.
Example: Microsoft Office suite (Word, Excel, PowerPoint).
Advantage: Increases perceived value and drives higher sales volumes.

4. **Platform (Market Place) Business Models**
Facilitates interactions between two or more groups (e.g., buyers and sellers).
Example: Airbnb connects property owners with travellers. Zomato, Swiggy connects restaurants with people.
Advantage: Scalable growth with low operating costs.

5. **Pay-as-You-Use Models** Customers are charged based on their usage rather than a flat fee.
Example: Amazon Web Services (AWS) charges based on computing power used.
Advantage: Attracts price-sensitive customers and optimizes resource utilization.

6. **Sharing Economy Model**

Users share access to goods or services, reducing individual ownership.

Example: Uber, Rapido for ridesharing.

Advantage: Low capital investment for businesses; cost savings for customers.

7. **Ecosystem Creation**

Building interconnected offerings that enhance each other.

Example: Apple's ecosystem of devices (iPhone, iPad, MacBook) and services (iCloud, Apple Music).

Advantage: Increases customer stickiness and lifetime value.

8.**Direct-to-Consumer (DTC) Models**

Brands bypass traditional retailers to sell directly to customers.

Example: Dollar Shave Club's subscription razor delivery service.

Advantage: Eliminates middlemen, reducing costs and fostering closer customer relationships.

9.Dynamic Pricing Model

Companies adjust cost of products/Services based on factors like demand, competition, and inventory levels.

Ex- Fluctuations of Flight Prices

Advantage: Generates more revenue.

10.Razor and Blade Model

Companies Sell a base product at a low cost (or at a loss) and make profits from consumables or complementary products.

Examples: Gillette razors and blades.

Printers and ink cartridges.

Advantage: Locks customers into a system, ensuring recurring revenue.

11.Franchise Model

Description: A business allows others to use its brand name, operational systems, and products for a fee or share of revenue.

Examples: McDonald's, Subway, Domino's.

Advantage: Rapid expansion with lower capital investment from the parent company.

12.Licensing Model

A company licenses its intellectual property (IP), technology, or brand to others for use, generating royalties or fees.

Examples: Disney licensing characters for merchandise.

Advantage: Generates passive income while expanding market reach.

13.Peer-to-Peer (P2P) Model

Allows individuals to interact directly with each other, bypassing intermediaries.

Examples: LendingClub (peer-to-peer lending). Tinder.

Advantage: Leverages community resources, reducing operational overhead.

14.Network Effect Model

The value of a product or service increases as more people use it.
Examples: Facebook, WhatsApp, LinkedIn.

15.Hidden Revenue Model

The primary product or service is offered for free, while revenue is generated indirectly.
Examples: Google (free search, revenue from ads).
YouTube (free content, ad revenue, and premium subscriptions).
Advantage: Attracts a large user base while monetising through third-party partnerships.

There are many more such business models. Since these are already being used by different companies, as an entrepreneur you might have to invent/innovate new business models as per your need.

By implementing these business model innovations, companies can redefine their competitive position, respond to shifting market dynamics, and achieve sustainable profit margins. Each model serves different needs, enabling businesses to align their strategy with market opportunities effectively.

PROCESS INNOVATION

Process innovation involves improving or redesigning internal workflows, procedures, or technologies to increase efficiency, reduce costs, improve quality, or speed up operations.

If you look at process innovation in terms of increasing profit margin, our only goal here is to reduce input costs as much as we can. There is nothing much that we can do that increases the customer's willingness to pay.

Rather than focusing on product itself, process innovation focuses on how to mass manufacture it and deliver it to the customers. This type of innovation often relies on adopting new tools, automating processes, or reorganising resources to optimise performance.

What Kind of Innovations Come Under This Category?

1. Automation

Using machines (Robots) or software to replace manual tasks.

Examples: Automobiles industry's automated production lines for vehicles.

2. Lean Manufacturing

Lean manufacturing is a production methodology focused on minimising waste within manufacturing systems while maximising productivity. It aims to create more value for customers with fewer resources by improving workflows, improving efficiency, and eliminating non-essential processes. (Read more about it to understand how to make manufacturing more efficient.)

Lean manufacturing originated from the Toyota Production System and is widely used across industries to reduce costs, improve quality, and respond quickly to changing demands.

3. Supply Chain Optimisation
Streamlining logistics and inventory management.
Examples: Mumbai Dabbawalla. Drone delivery by Zipline.

4. Process Standardisation
Creating uniform procedures to reduce variability and ensure consistent quality of products.
Examples: McDonald's standardised cooking processes for consistent quality helped them to scale globally.

5. Artificial Intelligence (AI) and Data Analytics
Using AI and Data Analysis for inventory management and prediction of demand.
Examples: McDonald uses AI to predict demand based on historical data, weather patterns, and local events to manage inventory at individual outlets.

Apart from these, there are other Process innovations that helps a company to increase efficiency and cut costs. Here are some of them-

1. Waste Reduction Initiatives
2. Outsourcing and Offshoring
3. Efficient allotment of Resources (Workforce, Machinery, Capital, Space) to different works.
4. Workforce Efficiency Enhancements
5. Predictive Maintenance
6. Hybrid work Models
7. Blockchain for process transparency

By focusing on process innovation, businesses can achieve substantial cost savings, improve their competitive edge, and respond faster to market demands. This innovation is especially critical for companies aiming to scale operations efficiently while maintaining quality.

INNOVATION IN MARKETING AND BRAND BUILDING

Marketing is the process of promoting and selling products or services to meet customer needs, using strategies like advertising, sales, and market research to drive growth.

Brand building is about creating a unique, memorable identity for a company, focusing on values, messaging, and customer experiences to foster loyalty and trust.

While marketing attracts customers, brand building creates lasting emotional connections and recognition, ensuring long-term success.

Innovation in marketing and brand building has three main goals. Our First goal is to reach to maximum possible people in minimum price, that is to keep the marketing cost low.
Our Second goal is to retain the customer.
Whether a customer will buy from the same company or not depends majorly on quality of the product, but to some extent, marketing may help in creating emotional connection.
Our third goal is to position the brand in such a way to increase the perceived value of the product so that Willingness to Pay (WTP) of the customer for a product increases. This helps us in generating more profit margin per sale.

Marketing and brand building is one area where we can use our creativity to maximum limit. Here are some innovative things that companies are doing in marketing and brand building that we can also do.

VIRAL CONTENT MARKETING

Viral content marketing involves creating highly shareable content like memes, social media posts and videos designed to spread quickly across social media and online platforms. The goal is to craft emotionally engaging, entertaining content that resonates with audiences, often using humour, controversy, or trending topics. This content generates large-scale attention in a short time, rapidly boosting brand visibility and engagement.

Innovative viral ads -

1. Man will be man by imperial blue
2. Indra nagar ka Gunda by CRED
3. Bold care ad feat. Johnny sins
4. Witty Twitter post and billboards by Zomato
5. Fogg chal rha he
6. Amul cartoon

MARKETING BY SECONDARY CONTENT

Secondary Content Marketing refers to the creation and distribution of content that provides lasting value to a specific audience over time. Unlike viral content, which is designed for immediate attention and rapid sharing, secondary content is intended to educate, inform, or engage the audience consistently. It typically focuses on solving problems, answering questions, or building trust, making it a foundational strategy for long-term brand growth and authority building.

Examples-

1. Varsity by Zerodha
2. WTF is Podcast by Nikhil Kamath (Zerodha)
3. The BarberShop by Shantanu (Bombay Shaving Company)
4. Design Tutorials by Canva
5. Running app by Nike and adidas
6. Talks at Google
7. CRED curious by CRED

DIGITAL TARGED ADs

A revolutionary innovation in advertising industry, Targeted ads are online advertisements delivered to users based on specific criteria such as their age, gender, education, interests, online behaviour, location etc. Unlike traditional advertising, which broadcasts messages to a broad audience, targeted ads focus on reaching potential customers more precisely, often across platforms like Facebook, Instagram, Google, Websites they visit or YouTube etc.

Advertisements are targeted based on the data collected from the user by various means. Based on this data, companies like Google and Facebook use AI and machine learning to match ads to users.

Why Has Targeted Advertising Been Revolutionary?

1. Increased Efficiency:

Targeted ads ensure that businesses reach the right audience, minimising wasted ad spend and increasing the chances of conversion.

2. Personalisation:

Ads are tailored to individual preferences and behaviour, making them more relevant and engaging for users.

3. Real-Time Optimisation:

Platforms continuously analyse campaign performance, enabling advertisers to tweak campaigns in real time for better results.

4. Cost-Effectiveness:

Businesses, especially small and medium-sized ones, can compete with larger companies by reaching niche audiences cost-effectively. And ROI in targeted ads in general is higher than other mediums.

5. Scalability:

Advertisers can easily scale campaigns to reach broader or more specific audiences based on campaign goals.

6. Cross-Platform Reach:

Targeted ads follow users across multiple platforms, ensuring consistent messaging and engagement wherever users are online.

7. Measurability:

Detailed analytics and performance reports provide insights into impressions, clicks, conversions, and ROI, helping businesses refine their strategies.

8. Global Accessibility:

Brands can reach audiences worldwide with targeted campaigns tailored to different demographics, languages, and cultures.

PERSONAL BRANDING

Personal branding has emerged as a powerful and innovative strategy for marketing and building a company's brand. By associating a leader's or key individual's persona with the business, companies can establish a strong connection with their audience, build trust, and differentiate themselves in the market.

Personal branding involves crafting and promoting the public image of an individual–such as a CEO, founder, or key team member–to reflect their expertise, values, and personality. This individual's brand is then closely aligned with the company's identity, making them a credible and relatable face of the organisation.

Elon Musk's personal branding as a visionary and risk-taking innovator significantly benefits his companies like Tesla and SpaceX by building trust, attracting massive media attention, and inspiring loyalty among customers, employees, and investors.

Musk's reputation as a forward-thinking entrepreneur who tackles global challenges (like sustainable energy and space exploration) builds credibility for his companies. And thus, owning a Tesla car often feels like being part of a revolutionary movement. Moreover, Tesla benefits significantly from Elon Musk's personal branding, which allows the company to spend far less on traditional marketing compared to competitors.

INNOVATION IN MARKETING AND BRAND BUILDING TO INCREASE THE PERCEIVED VALUE

In viral content marketing if our goal was to increase the number of people that recognise our brand and products. There we had to use our creativity to figure out "how and where to tell our message?" So that it reaches maximum people.
As far as "Innovation in marketing and brand building to increase the perceived value" is concerned our goal here is to position the product in such a way that increases the perceived value of the product and increase the willingness to pay (WTP) of consumer. Here we are more concerned with "what we tell in the message."

Here are some innovative marketing and brand-building techniques that increases the perceived value of their product.

1.Aspirational Brand Positioning

Example: Rolex positions itself as a symbol of success, sophistication, and achievement, making it an aspirational brand that consumers desire to own as a status symbol.

2. Exclusivity (Scarcity and Urgency)

Example: Nike creates artificial scarcity with its limited-edition sneakers, such as the Nike Air Jordans, which are produced in small quantities and are highly sought after by sneaker enthusiasts. This increases the perceived value of the product through exclusivity.

3.Legacy (Storytelling)

Example: Rolls-Royce leverages its rich history of engineering excellence and craftsmanship in its marketing, telling stories about its legacy of luxury, precision, and status, making the brand more desirable.

4. Artisan or Craftsmanship Branding

Example: Bose emphasises its superior engineering and attention to detail in its audio products. Known for high-quality sound and craftsmanship, the brand markets itself as a leader in premium sound, which increases the perceived value of its speakers and headphones.

5. Premium Pricing

Example: Apple's premium pricing strategy reinforces its positioning as a high-quality, cutting-edge brand. Consumers associate the higher price with superior technology, design, and brand prestige.

6. Iconic Visual Identity

Example: Nike has built an iconic visual identity through its famous "Swoosh" logo and "Just Do It" slogan. These elements have become synonymous with athletic excellence and empowerment, which enhances the brand's value.

7. Value-Based Marketing (Sustainability, Innovation)

Example: Tesla's focus on electric vehicles (EVs) has revolutionised the automobile industry. By positioning its cars as not only eco-friendly but also high-performance and innovative, Tesla has significantly increased the perceived value of its vehicles, associating sustainability with cutting-edge technology and luxury.

INNOVATION IN CUSTOMER EXPERIENCE

1. Customisation –

Rolls-Royce offers full customisation options, allowing customers to choose bespoke features like paint colours, wood types, and personalised interiors, making each car unique. This exclusivity attracts high-net-worth individuals, enables premium pricing, builds emotional connections, and fosters strong brand loyalty, resulting in higher margins and repeat business.

2. Personalisation –

Amazon uses AI to recommend products based on browsing and purchase history, while Netflix suggests content based on viewing behaviour and customised thumbnails for individual users. These strategies enhance customer satisfaction, increase engagement, boost conversion rates, and encourage long-term retention, driving higher sales and recurring revenue through subscriptions.

3. Post-Purchase Experience

(i) After-Sales Service: Despite having a good product, Ola in India is now infamous for having poor services, which is driving customers away from it. Good after sales service creates brand loyalty, Repeat sales and word of mouth publicity.

(ii) Repairability: Fairphone's modular design allows self-replacement of parts and easy repairs, appealing to eco-conscious customers, reducing e-waste, and enhancing brand loyalty.

(iii) Customer Support: With innovations like AI chat bots and Virtual assistant Companies are revolutionising customer support. They are available 24*7 and are cost-effective too.

4. Virtual Try-Ons -

Lenskart's AI-powered virtual try-on lets customers see how glasses will look on them before buying, enhancing convenience, increasing online sales by reducing purchase hesitation, and lowering return rates, which ultimately boosts profitability and customer satisfaction.

5. On-Time Delivery and Easy Returns
Amazon Prime offers ultra-fast delivery and hassle-free returns, driving customer satisfaction, membership sign-ups, and repeat purchases.
Blinkit and Zepto provide 10–20-minute grocery deliveries, addressing urban convenience needs, encouraging frequent high-volume purchases, and creating differentiation in a competitive market.
6. Community Building –
Royal Enfield fosters a strong rider community through events, bike rides, and exclusive merchandise, building emotional bonds with customers and turning them into brand advocates.

Summary

✦We can have higher margins by decreasing the input cost and increasing the perceived value of the product.

✦Both these goals can be achieved by INNOVATION. We discussed about five of them.

✦Innovation in Product/Service, which I think is the most important of all five. Using cutting edge technology to make new innovative product/services helps us to cut cost and also increases the perceived value. Innovation in product and services helps us to create unique products with intellectual property that helps us to get easier entry into the market, may help us in creating monopoly , also helps us to sustain in the market and can also become barrier to entry for others, and it can also help us to destroy the monopolies and duopolies.

✦Innovation in Business Model, like subscription model, freemium models, etc. helps us to maximise revenue and profit from the same products.

✦Process innovation practices like automation, lean manufacturing, supply chain optimisation, process standardisation can help us to cut cost.

✦Innovations in Marketing and Brand Building like content marketing, targeted ads, personalised branding, and marketing techniques like aspirational brand positioning, storytelling, creating scarcity and urgency etc. helps a brand to increase the perceived value and also increases sales volume by reaching to larger potential customers.

✦Innovation in customer experience like customisation, personalisation, post purchase experience etc. helps brands to create loyalty and increase sales and profit.

Chapter 5

The Disproportionate Income

In beginning of the book, we discussed about salaried employees and independent professionals and how their income dependent on number of hours they worked. We discussed how their income was proportional to time and that's what we had called proportionate income.

In this chapter, we will discuss about disproportionate income sources.

So, what is this disproportionate income?

Here I have given some features of the disproportionate sources of income.

1. Here income is <u>not a function of time</u>. Or at least you can say it's not a linear function of time. If I put in simpler words the income from these sources does not depend on (i)how many hours that person worked? (ii)Did he work every day or not? (iii)Did he work eight hours or not? Here Income does not depend on such things.
2.It does not depend (or depends less) on how many hours you yourself worked in a day.

3. There is no limitation on how high you can earn in a day.
4. The work you do once, that work keeps generating the income again and again; sometimes even forever. Even when you no longer work. Even when you have died.
5. The income here depends on quality of the work. Your income depends on the demand of your work, product or service you generate. Your income depends on your originality, creativity, uniqueness etc.

Now let's understand how does that work?

We will understand this by studying the 2 kinds of people who are earning this disproportionate income.

1. The Businesses

Businesses have been the age old, time-tested disproportionate sources of income.
We have already discussed how businesses overcome the limitation of time. Businesses reward the entrepreneur disproportionately for number of hours he worked.

We can understand this by looking at the establishment journey of businesses.

There are many works that an entrepreneur has to do to establish a successful business, here I am going to discuss two important works. These are the works that are rewarded disproportionately. Let's look at them one by one.

1. Research and Development

Product is the heart and soul of any company. The work that goes into Research and Development (R&D), that processes of invention/innovation of the products rewards the entrepreneur and the company disproportionately.

R&D generates intangible assets like patents, designs, chemical formula, software code, electronic circuit etc. We have already discussed about the invention and innovation and how do they give a company an upper hand. Here I would like to highlight that inventions and innovations keep giving recurring returns to the entrepreneur and his company for a very long time.

Coco cola is the best and most famous example. Even after more than hundred years, Coca-Cola's recipe remains guarded secret. Just think about the effort that went into making the Coca-Cola's formula and also calculate the return it has generated over the years.

This is the beauty of invention I am discussing about. Inventor did the work once and company is ripping its fruits till date and will continue to do so for many more years to come.

Your brain is real gold mine. If there is a way to create money out of thin air, it would be invention/innovation. The brain does not just give us billion-dollar business ideas, it can also create intangible assets which can give millions and billions of dollars of revenue.

As we discussed the story of Karsanbhai and Nirma, if a person is not born into a rich family or he/she does not have a lot of capital to invest; then invention and innovations can be your best bets to richness.

Another similar story is of world's Richest Man. This story is a prime example of how innovation can pave the way to wealth. Even when starting with limited resources in 1995, Elon Musk (24 years old then) and his brother Kimbal co-founded Zip2, their first major business. Their idea was to create software that would bring business directories and maps online for newspapers—an innovative idea at that time, when the internet was new. Recognising the potential of digital media, Musk saw an opportunity to help traditional newspapers embrace the internet.

With little financial backing, the Musk brothers lived in their office to save costs and devoted their time to build Zip2. Their persistence and unique solution eventually paid off when they secured contracts with major newspapers, including The New York Times.

By 1999, Compaq acquired Zip2 for $307 million, earning Musk $22 million in span of 4 years. This success provided Musk with thc resources to launch ventures like PayPal, Tesla, and SpaceX.
From sleeping in office in 1995 to sitting on pile of $22 million in 1999, Elon's story proves that by addressing real-world needs with creative innovative solutions, even those starting from modest beginnings can achieve remarkable financial success.

You have to put one time effort in making a revolutionary product with high enough margins, and it keeps generating the income as long as there is not a better and cheaper product in the market.

Although companies have a R&D department which keeps refining the existing product, so saying that invention and innovation are one-time effort, might not be 100% correct. A business has to keep continuously innovating to stay in the market. But the idea here is to highlight the fact that inventions and innovations gives way way way more returns in comparison to the time and investment that it took.

2. The System of Production and Sales

After doing all the R&D and making the final product. The next step is to mass produce it and sell it.

If businessman had a limitation to open only one factory or only one business, his/her income would have also been limited. But his income's growth possibility comes from ability to scale.

If he himself had to be present in every factory, every office, that he owns, he could not have scaled and never would have grown the business, and we would have never seen big business empires like Reliance, Tata, Adani, etc.

They can grow and establish such a large company because they put in place, what I call A **System of Production and Sales**.

What is this **System of Production and Sales**?

In order to mass produce a product, an entrepreneur puts in place the factory, machines and raw material. And he makes a team of people that operates those machines and tools to ultimately make the final goods and services.

The next task is to sell them, for which a team of sales and marketing is installed.

Hierarchy of managers is installed to keep the system of production and sales functioning smoothly.

As far as the system of production and sales is concerned, it involves more of repetitive tasks and less of creative tasks. Companies have a training department to train people for these tasks.

All the employees (either the part of production or sales team) are assigned a task and they complete for the individual or the company.

After establishment of the system, an entrepreneur's next target is to separate himself from this daily management of the system. They put in people to run this system. Entrepreneurs make sure that this system runs without them having to interrupt on day-to-day basis.

This is what is called to put the system on auto pilot.

Once the system is established, and it can run on its own; Entrepreneurs moves towards growing it. His next aim is to open another factory or open another company. After opening another factory, he puts that on auto pilot as well by same methodology.
They might focus on expanding in a new territory like Amazon did. Or they might focus on opening companies in other fields, like Mukesh Ambani did.

So, the idea here is that, when the system is established, it runs on its own with help of a hierarchy of managers. This system keeps generating income for the entrepreneur, even when he himself has stopped working or doesn't work as hard.

It is this system that grows and becomes bigger, and entrepreneur's asset also keeps increasing.
Example - The price of one Google share in 2015 (when Sundar Pichai took over) was around $32 which has now increased to $162. Despite Larry page (cofounder of Google) not actively working at Google anymore.

Apart from that, a businessman also opens multiple companies in his lifetime. People wonder "We couldn't open a single company yet, but here is a guy who is opening companies after companies".
What we need to understand here is that once a businessman understands that a factory, an office, a company can successfully run without him. He starts replicating these factories, offices, and companies. He takes a loan, hires some people, and starts a company and puts it on auto pilot as well. And this way he keeps earning money from various ventures.

Before you become overcharged, let me tell you both this tasks (product R&D, and establishment of the system of production and sales) is not so easy. An entrepreneur has to work really hard and smart to finish these tasks.

I have given information about all the tasks that an entrepreneur has to do to establish this system of production and sells in next Chapter.

But what we need to understand here is that the work that an entrepreneur docs in product development and establishment of this system, rewards the entrepreneur disproportionately.

All the rich nations know the power of invention. Some invest as high as 4 to 5% of their GDP for research and development. Unfortunately, India spends only 0.2% of GDP on research and development.
According to a report by *THE HINDU*, in FY2023, India witnessed 83,000 patents being filed. Whereas according to the World Intellectual Property Organisation (WIPO), In 2023, the number of patent applications filed by residents in United States was at 518,364.
More about this, I will discuss in chapter "How a country can get rich?"

Second way to generate disproportionate income:

The Content Creator Way

The world is filled with countless industrial products—ranging from cars and electronic devices to chemical products like soaps, cosmetics, and even software and websites. The development of these products relies heavily on various branches of engineering. From electronics and software engineering to chemical engineering, material sciences, nanotechnology, biotechnology, and mechanical engineering. Each field plays a crucial role in creating innovative solutions. When we think of invention or innovation, the first thing that often comes to mind is a tangible product born from these disciplines.

But here, in this chapter we are taking a broader view of invention and innovation. For me anything which is an original creation is invention. It includes films, YouTube videos, audios, songs, books, art forms, poems, stories, a code, a circuit, an app, everything is an invention which is uniquely made.

Whereas inventing and innovating an industrial product and mass producing it, requires a factory and a company. Some of these second category of innovative products like- YouTube videos, Songs, Books, Smartphone Apps etc. can be made by an individual. We can call such people Solopreneur in true sense. Here we will just call them “Creators”.

<u>Creation of these things is our second source of generating disproportionate income.</u>

In rest of the chapter we will understand, how these products generate disproportionate income?

We can understand this by an example.

You wrote a book of poems. A person buys your book and reads your poems. Yet the copies of your books can be purchased and read by another one million people and yet again by infinite number of people.

Book publishers might need to print the copies but at least You don't have to keep writing the poems for every single reader. You wrote the book once, now it can be sold to millions and billions of people.

If you are selling in form of digital copies (i.e. e-books), even the publisher does not have to print the copies again and again.

If I say this in terms of economics, there is no marginal cost of production here. You make something once, you ripe the fruits forever.

Once you have written a book and a person buys it, you get money. You keep getting money as long as people are buying it.

This is true for all such creations like movies, YouTube videos, audio songs, books etc.
Since these are assets which are giving you recurring income, you can call them digital assets.

You made a YouTube video and even if thousands or millions of people have watched it. It does not diminish the video in anyway. It can yet again be watched by other billions of the people.

This book or the video generate disproportionate income in the sense that your income from this video does not depend on how many hours you took to make the video. But your income depends on the quality of the content. It depends on how creative you have been in the video; it depends on your originality. You earn because of how useful that video is, or how entertaining it is or how engaging it is.

Obviously, making a better video takes more time than making a bad one. But the beauty lies in the fact that once you make the video and uploads it, it keeps generating income without you having to work again and again for every single user.

Which is not true for any professional like lawyer, doctor or a teacher. They have to work again and again for each of their client, patient or student respectively.

The availability of Internet has further enhanced the possibility of generating high income by doing such disproportionate income generating works. Internet provides a platform and a medium of distribution for such products. Via Internet, a person sitting in random corner of a village in India can sell his digital products like e-books songs, podcasts, videos, courses, apps etc. to customers in any other corner of the world.

There is YouTube where you can upload your videos. There is App Store and Google's Play store where you can upload your apps. There are platforms where you can sell your e-books and physical books. There is Spotify and so many other platforms where you can put your songs and podcasts.

Putting your works out there on Internet gives you opportunity to have millions of customers. And as we had seen previously, number of customers is directly proportional to your income.

The fact that you don't have to work again and again for every consumer and, there is availability of millions and billions of customers online, to whom you can deliver, your product directly creates a possibility to generate very high income.

Which is not possible for most salaried employees and individual professionals because they have to be literally present with their employer and clients to deliver their service.

We may like it or not but the most fundamental science that is mathematics is working in favour of YouTubers and Instagram influencers which is giving them high income. And in order to get rich, mathematics must work in your favour.

This is the beauty of Inventions.
These are your disproportionate lines of income.

Not having Marginal Cost of Production in itself is a superpower. In 2005, Lakshmi Mittal was the richest person in the world. His company, ArcelorMittal, was the largest steel-producing company in the world, which is a remarkable achievement. However, in the steel business, you have to produce steel repeatedly for each customer, meaning there is a significant Marginal Cost of Production.

On the other hand, once you create software, you can copy and paste it to run on all computers or smartphones all over the world, resulting in almost negligible Marginal Cost of Production. This is why, Lakshmi Mittal was replaced by Bill Gates as the richest person in the world. He sold his Windows operating system (a software) globally in huge numbers. Even today, approximately 75% of the computers worldwide run on Microsoft Windows operating system.

Having marginal cost of production, doesn't mean the business is too bad. As of 29/1/2025 Lakshmi Mittal is world's 136th richest person, which is also great. Forbes

Just choose the businesses which have lower marginal cost of production.

It's just mathematics, you can have opinions about other viewpoints, but there is no place for opinions in maths. It's hardcore truth.

The price of anything in economy depends on demand and supply. Definitely, there is sufficient supply of doctors, engineers, teachers, lawyers, and other professionals. At a place where there is limited supply, their fees would be higher. But definitely, there is very little supply of inventors, innovators and entrepreneurs. And that is why these are the people who are being rewarded highly.

Creators and innovators work once and create something useful for all of humanity and keep getting the recurring income.

As Warren Buffett famously said, "If you don't find a way to make money while you sleep, you will work until you die." Disproportionate sources of income earn money for you while you sleep, in both the cases. As in case of entrepreneur, your factory can function while you sleep, your products get sold, even while you sleep. And in case of solopreneur, that is our content creator, even when he has gone to bed, his videos can be watched, his books can be read, his mobile apps can be downloaded and used by people.

This is the beauty of disproportionate lines of income where you work once, and you have recurring income. You need such a recurring income generator in order to become rich. These are the ways to make unlimited money (or High Income) out of limited 24 hours.

If you don't have money, create something original from what you have (your brain) and world buys it, world pays for it.

Challenges of Disproportionate Sources of Income

This chapter would be incomplete if I don't discuss about the other side of disproportionate sources of income.

In a proportionate source of income, if a person is earning ₹800 for doing eight hours of work, then in disproportionate sources of income, in his lifetime he might get ₹80,000 or ₹8 lakhs of rupees or even more for eight hours of work. But we cannot ignore the other side of the disproportionate income. Since income is not dependent on number of hours worked, this can also mean differently.

You might work 8 hours and still end up getting no money. Since this income sources rewards disproportionately, getting no rewards for doing a lot of work is also example of disproportionate income.

For disproportionate sources of income, If there is no maximum limit on the amount that can be earned in a day, there is also no minimum guaranteed income in the day, like salaried employees.

When you are setting yourself to earn via disproportionate sources of income, basically, you are throwing yourself into the jungle, that is market.

No matter how hard you worked, how much capital you invested, how many people you employed; if people(market) do not like your product or the service, all your efforts might give zero returns.

You can understand that by taking the example of movies. Directors, producers invest crores of rupees and make movies. They hire actors, shoot the movies, then marketing, and everything. But at the end of the day, if it's a good movie, then they earn the money. They earn disproportionately in the sense that they earn when it is screened in cinema hall. They earn the money when people watch it on OTT platforms like Netflix. They earn the money when it is streamed on TV. They keep earning years after they had made the movie.
Ex- Interstellar was once again released on 10th anniversary and once again made more than $10 million.
But frequently we also come across movies, which flops miserably. Kangana Ranaut's movie Dhaakad on day eighth of its release had sold only 20 tickets in all over India.

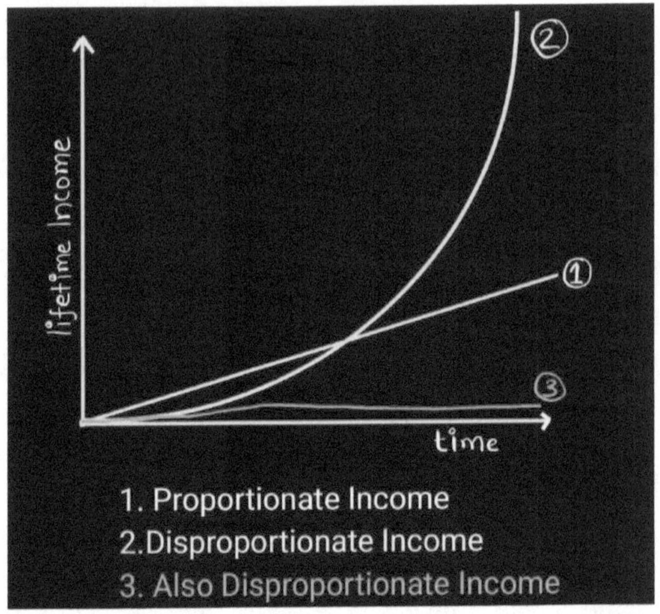

You can spend hours in making a YouTube video, and it might end up getting less than hundred views. You can start a business, and your products might end up not getting sold.

I acknowledge the possibility of failure. But personally, I am bullish on disproportionate sources of income. My idea is that you keep making products, one after another. It is not guaranteed that every work of yours will be successful, but even if some of them become successful, they will generate enough income to compensate for the rest of the failures. This is same as investors investing in a start-up. Majority of them will fail. It's about those 4 to 5% start-up that gives 10,000% or even more returns.

On the other hand, there are also people like CEOs, and other high skilled people who works on salary (basically earning proportionate to time) but their per day salaries are so high that they become richer than majority of people.

There is also example of sports personalities, who earn proportionate to their time, but their per hour income is so high that they are richer than majority of the population.

So, the bottom line is, earn extremely high if you want to earn proportionately.

The Freelancers and the Shopkeepers

Anyways Here I would like to discuss about the interesting case of the Freelancers and shopkeepers.

Let's first start with the freelancer, they have an illusion that they are their own boss.

First of all, let's be clear. They are not their own Boss. They also have a deadline from their client to finish the work. They also get a fixed income from their clients. Probably the only advantages they have are that they can take leave whenever they want and work whenever they feel like.

However, as far as their income is concerned, their income equation is not very much different than a salaried employee.

Let's understand this by taking example of a freelancer -
1. He is paid on hourly basis. And We already know what disadvantages are of getting paid on hourly basis. Same limitation of having 24 hours in a day is applied to the income of freelancer.
2. A freelance does not get recurring income from working once.
3. He has to get up every day and work to earn every day.
So, what we are seeing is that a freelancer is a contractual employee, who just like salaried employee is finishing the tasks for the entrepreneur. They don't earn like business owners; they earn like employees.

So, they are not their own boss, they are just their own employees.

A better alternative is to become solopreneur, the creator, who earns disproportionately.

Now let's discuss about the Shopkeepers. They have an illusion that they are also businesspeople. While I know some of the shopkeepers who are quite rich, but at max, we can call these shopkeepers as traders, but not businesspeople.

Why am I saying this?

We can understand this by analysing the income of a shop owner who himself sits in the shop to sell his inventory.

1. The biggest disadvantage is that they themselves have to be present at the shop to keep it functioning. With his inability to be absent, comes the inability to scale. If his shop requires him to be present, then he cannot open another shop, because even that shop will require him to be present there. In such a case he cannot scale. That is to say in future, he cannot have 1 to 2, 2 to 4 and 4 to 8 shops.
2. He has no intellectual property to defend his business. Anybody with enough capital can open shop nearby his shop and destroy his revenue.
3. With not having any intellectual property of himself, he cannot charge high margins.
4. Shopkeepers don't generate recurring income. They have to open shop every day to earn every day.
5. They have a smaller customer base if they are not selling it online.
6. They are not earning while they sleep.

Here are some suggestions that they can implement to increase their income-

A) Start selling online also to have larger customer base.
B) Follow the models of Reliance retail and Zudio. If you see, after all, these are also shops but Mukesh Ambani or Tatas do not have to be present in their stores to sell their goods. They have set up a system. These stores have some feature that helps them to run these stores on auto pilot.
Here are some features of these superstores that shop owners should follow-
1. All the products have a fixed price, there is no room for bargaining.
2. Technology- POS machines for billing. An employee can handle money and billing. Owner is not needed for this.
3. CCTV cameras, helping the owner to have a watch all the time.

Where there are not these three things, there is a great disadvantage. The disadvantage is that if there is any scope of bargaining, you cannot trust any employee in such a case. He might sell goods at a different price and will tell the employer a different price. In such a case the shopkeeper himself will have to be present at billing counter. But if the shopkeeper himself has to be present in the shop, then the business cannot be scaled. He cannot open 1 to 2, 2 to 4 shops.

But if the price of the product is fixed, and there is no scope of bargaining, the shopkeeper himself need not be present in the shop. He can employ a guy for the billing purposes and the shop can be put on autopilot. That's what these big stores do. If a shopkeeper also applies this to his shop, then his shop can also be run without him, and definitely the business can be scaled.

There are many other systems to micromanage the operations of these superstores. But I don't want to get into that you can search about that on Internet. This system gives advantage to the owner to replicate the same store elsewhere. Which helps the owner to grow and expand. By growth and expansion only even a shopkeeper successfully opens one to 2, 2 to 4 and 4 to 8 shops then only he can be called businessman in true sense.

Summary

- Features of Disproportionate Sources of income- (i) Income from these sources is independent from the no. of hours worked. (ii) There is no limitation on how high you can earn. (iii) You work once, and that work keeps generating the income again and again. (iv) The income here depends on quality of the work.
- 2 ways to generate disproportionate income. (i) The Business way(ii) The Creator way.
- In Business, Innovation (R&D) give high and repeated returns.

✦System of Production and Sales helps a businessman to put his business on autopilot and thus freeing him to grow and scale his business.

✦Creators (authors, YouTubers, musicians, filmmakers etc.) earns disproportionately because their work can he consumed by whole of humanity without them having to work for every single consumer again and again.

✦Disproportionate sources of income come with risk of complete failure and may not generate any income at all. Also, high skilled people (although earning proportionately) become richer than majority of population.

✦A freelancer's income equation is also just like salaried employees (dependent on time). And come with an upper ceiling.

✦If a shop owner himself has to be present in his shop to run, then he cannot scale his business. They should copy supermarket model to scale their business.

Chapter 6

Your Pathway to Become Rich

We started this book with a criticism for salaried jobs. However, I would say not everyone might be interested in doing business or being a creator, and if you are one of those who want to do the job, then I would ask you to do the high skilled jobs that pays well.

But if you are one of those who want to earn the disproportionate income, then, as we seen in the last chapter that there are two ways, and we will explore these two ways and try to find a path that can be followed.

The Business Way

Once you have decided that you want to be an entrepreneur, then next question that arises is what business should I do? Or how do I do it?

I have divided the whole journey of building a business in four parts, those are- The Scientist, The Founder, The CEO and The Chairperson.

The Scientist

By scientist, I don't mean a science graduate or a person who has deep knowledge about science. By scientist here, I mean the innovator, the problem solver, the visionary, who picks a problem and find a solution to it.

As we had already discussed in order to sell something to the others, the product or the service should solve some of their problem or simply make them feel good. So, in order to build a business first step is to SEE A PROBLEM. A problem which you, yourself have faced or people around you faced.

Research about this problem Ask yourself and people around you, how big is the problem?
How many other people faces it?
Can I solve it?
Will people pay money for solution of this problem?
And how much they can pay?
How big is the market? etc.
Do the market research about these questions.

Elon musk has divided the problems in four categories-

1. Large problem of large population
2. Small problem of large population
3. Large problem of small population
4. Small problem of small population

As Elon says, the first category of problems (the large problem of large population) is the best to work on. And then small problem of large population.

If the problem is large, the product can be priced higher and if this problem is faced by large population, then this large problem is our potential customer base.

(By the way, lack of money is a big problem for a large population, which this book tries to address)

Anyways, back to the topic.

If you cannot find a large problem of large population, then second choice is small problem of large population.

Why choose a small problem of large population? For two reasons: -

1. If it's a small problem, solving this problem might be easier and it would need less capital (investment), less machinery and less people to solve it.
2. If a large population of people faces this problem, then here also, we can have a large customer base and as we have already seen number of customers is directly proportional to money earned.

It's best example is Paytm, which started as a platform to recharge our mobile phones. Which was a small problem. Today, in order to recharge your phone, they charge very small fees of ₹1 to ₹2, Which might appear as a very small amount to you but remember that population of India is 140 crore and more than half of the people use mobile phones. In such a case even if 30-40 crore people use platform like Paytm to recharge their mobile phone then that would result in more than ₹30 - 40 crore of monthly revenue for PayTm.

People have also built successful businesses around the "Large problem of Small people" or "Small problem of Small people", especially when that small group is of the people with large money; basically, The Rich.

The best example of this is Bernard Arnault. Who had become world's richest man sometime ago. His companies Louis Vuitton (LVMH) and others make luxury goods. These products do not seem to be solving a real problem. They just help rich to look rich.

Anyways, once you have picked the problem and set yourself on a journey to solve the problem, our first task is to make the product or service that solves the problem.

This is where the scientist part of an entrepreneur is required.

The best-case scenario is, you yourself can make the product. It is only possible when you have the right skills. Sometimes in order to solve a problem, you have to completely invent or innovate the product. And that may require technical skills like coding, product design, circuit design, knowledge of physics and maths and chemistry etc. That's where being an engineer comes handy.

This is also the reason why many founders are engineers. Henry Ford, Mark Zuckerberg, and Elon musk. It gives an edge in a way that when you have the idea, you can start working on it all alone.

Does that mean all those who are not engineers or those who do not have technical skills cannot be founders/entrepreneurs?

The answer is no, there are many entreprencurs who do not know much about the technology but are successful entrepreneurs.

A person who wants to develop a product, but doesn't know how to make, he/she can always hire some engineers/researchers to make the product for him. But in such a case, you need capital to pay these engineers/researchers.
For example- Mukesh Ambani is not an AI scientist but JIO is developing AI model in collaboration with IIT Bombay.

We have another example of Steve Jobs, Steve Jobs is credited with the idea of the iPhone, but definitely he did not write the code or designed the circuits. They were the engineers at Apple who made the iPhone. But what we need to understand here is Apple had capital to pay to these engineers, that's why Steve Jobs could realise his vision.

Which gives rise to a question. A person who does not have technical knowledge and also doesn't have capital to hire somebody else to do the research work; Can he not dream to become an entrepreneur?

Well, here is also a way out here. If a person is visionary enough, but he is not a tech guy and doesn't have capital to finance the research as well. Then, in such a case, ask the engineer/technical guy to be the co-founder. And offer him equity in the company.

Pro tip- Visit Science Project Competitions. You might find the guy to work with. Or you may get all three; a new idea, a new product, and a guy to work with. Obviously if he/she agrees to work with you.

Additionally, you yourself may organise a project competition or a hackathon, keep a prize money and ask the contestant to develop a product to solve a particular problem. Later you can start a company with the winner.

If you cannot find the cofounder as well, then the last resort is to Learn the skill to make the product. More about this in chapter number 7(Education to Get Rich).

One question that I would like to address here is, do you necessarily need to quit your college or job till this stage of entrepreneurship?

The answer is No. As many people have said and I agree that, up to this stage, you need not leave your job. You should first make Minimum Viable Product (MVP), that means a version of the product that just gets the things done.

And for developing MVP, you need not quit your college or job. You can do that at home, after your college or office hours.

Once the MVP is developed, our next step is mass production. This requires laying down the foundation for functional, efficient, and scalable manufacturing facility. Which takes us to our second step.

The Founder

In this step the entrepreneur is required to establish the System of the production and sales.
Establishing the System of manufacturing does not just include establishing factory and offices, but it

also involves a comprehensive set of tasks that ensure your product can be produced consistently, cost effectively and at a quality that meets market standards.

So here I have written the processes, tasks and sub tasks that can be followed to establish the system for efficient production and long-term growth. Depending on the industry some steps, tasks, subtasks might change here and there but major things will be same.

1. Company Naming, Branding, and Legal Setup

- Choose and Register the Company Name
- Design Brand Elements (Logo, Slogan, Colours)
- Register Trademarks and Patents
- Decide on Legal Structure (LLC, Corporation, Partnership)
- Register the Business Entity and Obtain Necessary Licenses
- Secure Business Insurance (liability, property, worker's compensation).

2. Securing Funding and Financial Planning

- Determine Initial Capital Requirements
- Secure Funding (Self-funding, Loans, Investors, Venture Capital)
- Prepare Financial Documents (Business Plans, Projections)
- Set Up Business Bank Accounts

- Establish Financial Systems (Accounting Software, Payment Processes)
- Allocate Budget for Different Departments

3. Location Selection and Site Acquisition

- Research Suitable Locations (Proximity to Resources, Transportation, Labour)
- Negotiate and Finalise Purchase or Lease Agreements
- Obtain Necessary Zoning and Construction Permits

4. Factory Design & Infrastructure Development

- Hire Architects and Civil Engineers for Factory Layout
- Design Office Spaces, Production and Storage Areas
- Keep in mind the Plan for Future Expansion
- Implement Safety and Security Measures (Surveillance, Fire Alarms, Fencing etc.)

5. Procurement of Machinery and Equipment

- Research and Compare Suppliers and Technologies
- Negotiate Purchase Terms (Cost, Delivery, Warranties)
- Oversee Delivery, Installation, and Calibration
- Set Up Maintenance Agreements with Equipment Suppliers
- Implement IT Systems and required software.

6. Workforce Planning and Hiring

• Develop Organisational Structure (Key Departments, Hierarchy)

• Recruit and Interview Candidates for Managerial and Key Positions (Production, HR, Finance, IT)

• Onboard and Train Key Staff (Factory Managers, Supervisors, Engineers)

• Establish Payroll, Benefits, and Employee Policies

7. Raw Material Sourcing and Transportation

• Establish Supply Contracts (Pricing, Quality Standards, Delivery Timelines)

•Establish Partnerships with Logistics Companies for Delivery

• Set Up Systems for Inventory Tracking and Management

8. Launching Initial Production and Trial Runs

The CEO Phase

After the foundation phase, next task is to run the company and get the output (product or service) and also sell it.

I have called it, the CEO phase.

It is the phase when the entrepreneur (CEO) has to manage a lot of things and also grow the company at the same time. Initially when the company is small and no. of employees is less, there are only 1-2 factories and offices, The CEO himself can manage a lot of things. But as the company grows it becomes humanly impossible to engage with every employee and personally assign them the work and look after every task.

Thats where hierarchy and delegation become important. Certain departments and key posts are created in the company. Under them The Entrepreneur tries to free himself from some of the works and duties so that he/she can focus on more important tasks.

On this basis I have divided the work of CEO under this phase into two categories.
Category 1 and Category 2.

The basis of division is whether the work can be delegated or not. Work which the entrepreneur has to do in initial phase of the company, but over time can be delegated to the responsible specialised employees are put under category one.

Works which an entrepreneur has to do in initial as well as later phase of the company, these works are usually not delegated and are of strategic importance, they are put under category two.

Category 1

Category one comprises the work that are related with day-to-day operations of the company. When the company is new and no. of employees is less, no. of managers is less or zero, and things are happening at a smaller scale; so, the entrepreneur is highly involved in managing and overseeing almost all of the works of company. But nature of these works is such that if a person is specialised in one particular task than, these works can be delegated to responsible employees. Works and tasks in this category involve responsibilities and tasks focused on daily functioning and management or business. It deals with execution of processes (rather than planning), ensuring that organisation runs smoothly on day-to-day basis.

Here are some of the most important works and tasks that falls under category 1-

1. Operations/production management
2. Human resource management
3. Sales and marketing
4. Day to day Finance work
5. Supply chain and inventory management
6. Research and development
7. Infrastructure management
8. Customer support
9. Administration
10. Legal and compliance

These are some of the verticals and departments that needs to be managed. Overtime different posts are created in the organisation like Chief Operating Officer (COO), Chief Marketing Officer (CMO), Chief Financial Officer (CFO), Chief Technical Officer (CTO), Chief Human Resourcc officer (CHRO), etc. These are the people who heads a particular department and handles tasks if thet department along with their subordinates.

CEO is the main leader who puts forward the target and coordinates with all these people and run the company.

Each of these verticals under this category, from sales and marketing to Operations, finance and R&D requires years of work to learn them. And enough literature has already been written about them you can easily get that. And if you are serious about being an entrepreneur then you should take out some time and study these subjects in detail.

Category 2

This involves works which an entrepreneur has to do in initial as well as later phase of the company. In fact, an entrepreneur frees himself from works of category 1 by delegating them to others so that he can focus on works of category two. This category involves the works which are of strategic importance. These are the responsibilities and activities focused on long-term planning, decision-making, and the overall direction of the organisation. These are concerned with how the company will grow, adapt, and thrive in a competitive landscape.

I have divided the works under category two into some subcategories as well. Here are they-

Strategic vision, planning, and Leadership

1. Defining vision, mission, core purpose, and values
2. Setting long-term objectives and goals
3. Developing growth strategy
4. Making key decisions
5. Analysing market trends and customer behaviour
6. Understanding industry, trends, and competitor actions

Financial oversight

1. Budgeting and cost control
2. Cash flow monitoring
3. Securing Investment and funding

Innovation and expansion

1. Launching new products
2. Market expansion and diversification
3. Exploring new revenue streams
4. Making deals, partnerships and acquisitions

Corporate management

1. Establishing governance structures

2. Engaging with key stakeholder like board of directors, investor, team members etc.

Overall Oversight

1. Not micromanaging but keeping an eye on what is happening in different departments of company.
2. Implementing standard operating procedure (SOPs)
3. Check Performance by key performance indicators (KPIs)

Public relation and brand building

1. Building a public image of company
2. Representing company in media. Participating in talks, podcast, and shows
3. Reputation management. Addressing customer feedback. Monitoring public perception.

The Chairperson

As far as this phase is concerned, there is no hard and fast rule. In this phase, we are discussing about the time when the entrepreneur steps down from CEO post and make somebody else the CEO. For example, as we have seen in case of Microsoft, Google, etc. Who made Satya Nadala and Sundar Pichai as the CEOs. However, there might be many entrepreneurs who likes to be the commander of their ship and may not step down. For example, Mukesh Ambani.

So, it's not necessary that the entrepreneur steps down from the top job, but if he does then we would like to see what his roles and responsibilities might look like.

1. In this role, the entrepreneur becomes more of a mentor and advisor, ensuring the company's long-term vision and values are upheld while allowing the management team to handle operational responsibilities.
2. They might be interested in Heading the board of directors and set long-term goals and objectives.
3. Monitor the performance of the CEO and senior management team, providing support and feedback as needed.
4. Maintain relationships with major stakeholders, including investors, customers, and community leaders.
5. Engage in Philanthropic and CSR activities.
6. Invest in other growing start-ups.

The Content Creator way

After the business way, another way to earn disproportionately is the content creation way. In This chapter, we will be looking at some ways how to earn by content creation?

First thing that we need to understand is that, probably videos are the most loved form of content.

YouTube videos, movies, podcast, online courses, stock videos are good sources of income. But we need to understand that other forms of content can also become good source of disproportionate income.

Here I have given different forms of the content that earns disproportionately-

Audio - songs, podcast, audiobooks.
Video - YouTube videos, movies, podcast, online courses, stock videos
Text - books, e-books, blogs, paid newsletters, online journals, magazines, articles, tweets.
Apps- Mobile apps, computer apps, video games
Photos - stock photos, wallpaper, icons, themes, templates and designs for websites, graphic designs, artwork etc.
Others- Online Communities, Social Media pages, online webinars and workshops, virtual goods in games and there are many more.

There are different platforms to sell these products, you can find about them on internet.

Ok. So as far as content creation is concerned, we can discuss about a lot of things, but I will confine myself on two topics.
(i) How to Grow and Engage the audience
(ii) How to earn more being a content creator?

How to Grow and Engage the audience?

1. Solve some problem- Being a creator also you have to solve some problem of your audience. You need to add some value in lives of your audience. When a writer writes a book or article it intends to help or teach something. You might argue that "I have seen cringe content creator, and they make a lot of money, what problem do they solve? "To some extent you are right but actually even this people are entertaining in some way. Even if they are not entertaining yet Most Human beings need something to divert their attention from real world pain, probably these cringe content creators provide that escape and that's why these cringe content creators are surviving. So, in a way they are also solving some problem.

2. Choose your niche- Based on your Passion, skills and Market demand choose a niche. It helps you to fulfil the demand of the audience who likes a particular type of content. Once that loyal audience base is built it becomes easier to monetise. Being different matters more than being the best. Find a niche or angle that makes your content stand out. You can choose something unusual as well. For example, combine two interests that may seem unrelated (e.g., technology and meditation) and create content that uniquely connects them.

3. Be an expert in your field- Being an expert makes you stand out. It helps greatly if you are a writer, musician, artist etc. You might have seen many old people on internet with huge fan following. They are the people who were building their skills when nothing like Internet existed at their place, and I don't think they had any idea one day they might get international fame. But despite that they worked on their skill, and it is rewarding them. So yes, Having skill and expertise help.

4. Upload even if nobody is watching right now- if you consistently upload your content, even if you are not getting views, it's okay. If one of your video get viral, then the public will have bunch of other related content to consume and eventually all of your other content will also get views.

5. Personal Branding- Establish a unique voice and identity. Focus on relationship building, not just followers.

Some other tips-

1. Be consistent
2. Learn Search engine optimisation (SEO) and make your content more discoverable.
3. Collaborate with other content creators, if that works for you.
4. Use multiple platforms
5. Create or translate your content into multiple languages.

How to have more income being a content creator?

1. Have Multiple monetisation method- Do not depend on one platform or one revenue stream. For example, if you are a YouTuber, combine ad revenue with affiliate marketing, sponsorships, merchandise, and direct sales of products.

2. Create Complementary Products: If you make educational videos, create, and sell e-books or courses that delve deeper into your topics.

3. Introduce Subscription Model: Launch a membership program on platforms like a YouTube, Patreon or through your own website. Offer exclusive members only content, early access etc. Subscription models bring in consistent, recurring revenue, which is crucial for long-term success.

4. Paid Consulting or Webinar: Once you establish yourself as an expert in a particular field, you can offer nuanced, in-depth knowledge via personal consulting or paid webinar.

5. Scale: as an individual, your time in a day is limited. As your audience grows and need for content creation rises, build a team of people for assisting you in various ways.

Summary

✦ We tried to find a path to richness.

✦ In the business way, we looked at four phases.

✦ In The Scientist Phase, an entrepreneur has to develop a solution to a problem.

✦ In The Founder Phase, the entrepreneur is supposed to establish a system of production and sales.

✦ In The CEO Phase entrepreneur is expected to successfully run and grow the company. Delegation and leadership are keys here.

✦ Later the entrepreneur might be interested in stepping down.

✦ In the content creation way, use the right strategy to grow your audience and increase your income.

Chapter 7

Education to Get Rich

Tarun and his co-founder Swapnil Jain came up with the idea for Ather energy all the way back in 2009 when they were students at IIT Madras and later on in 2013 they registered ather energy as a company with the goal of building the first ever made in India indigenous electric scooter. They secured ₹65 lakhs ($100,000) as seed funding from IIT Madras Incubation Cell and other investors.

In 2015, Ather Energy secured $1 million in funding from Sachin Bansal and Binny Bansal, the co-founders of Flipkart. This investment gave them the boost needed to accelerate development. And with that money they were able to create a low-speed electric scooter the s340. But this product was not up to the mark. So, they launched the Ather 450 which was the most powerful scooter in India at that time. They later launched 450x, 450s,450 Apex and Rizta.

Cut to present times, In CY2023 they sold more than 1,00,000 units, and registered a growth of 101%. They are now exporting their scooters to other countries as well. And soon they will be a public company.

Elon musk has similar story. He is a scientist. On paper also he is the chief engineer at SpaceX.

Earlier we discussed about Karsanbhai Patel, the founder of Nirma washing powder.

You will notice that many people despite coming from humble backgrounds, specialised in science and technology, and invented or innovated something and sold it to masses eventually became rich.

If I ask this question, how many Indians are educating themselves to be inventors or innovators? (I might discuss about India in between, as I am from India. However, on average, same things are applicable globally.)

Sadly, though those who are doing their master's and PhD are more interested in becoming assistant professors, rather than the research itself.

According to the All-India Survey on Higher Education (AISHE) 2021-22, 24.16 lakh students graduated with BA courses in India. Tell me what great product that degree helps us to make. It has its own relevance, but as far as economy is concerned these courses have not helped India.

Leave BA how many inventions and innovations our science/tech/engineering graduates are doing?

Unfortunately, our education has failed to create a lot of innovators and inventors.

Current education system is good at making people labours and majority of graduates are interested in getting a job that pays well. Basically, we want to be expensive labours.

We do all the difficult courses so that we can get those high packages. Surprisingly enough, those high packages are also celebrated in media.

So, to create wealth, I envisage education which focus on making inventors and innovators. Education which trains people to be problem solvers. People who pick up a problem and provide an innovative solution, and not just that they also build a successful business around it, and the best-case scenario would be to also export those product and services abroad as well.

The purpose must be well defined for engineering graduates that you are here to learn the problems solving abilities. You are here to learn the cutting-edge technologies and later use those technologies to make innovative product and services that makes life easier and eventually create wealth.

R&D and innovation has always been the gold mine of wealth and that's why education, especially the higher education, the professional education has to shift its goal from labour maker to inventor maker.

And here, I do not want to sound like a critic of education system. And if you are also one of those solution-oriented guys, I would ask you not to indulge in system criticism as well.

Fixing the whole system is government's job and they will do it at their own pace.

We can focus on things at our own level. Our own education.

Ask yourself - How can I educate myself that will be financially rewarding? What are the skills I need to learn, what are the courses I need to take to specialise or to get knowledge about one particular field, technology or problem?

Once you have selected a problem to work on and if you start looking at the solutions, even if you don't know what is the solution, you can research more about it and learn the skill what needs to be learnt and if you keep moving towards the solution. Eventually you will get it.

I have given an example here; in this example I have shown the journey from picking up a problem to looking for a solution and how to educate yourself to solve the problem.

For example – sugar candies are sold at very large scale in India and almost all of them are consumed by children which affect their health negatively.

In such a situation, you would like to buy a healthier trophy for your kids, but there are not so many healthier alternatives available at affordable prices.

In such a situation you think of making healthier alternatives, but you don't know "how to make toffees? "

The next step would be to learn how to make toffees? if you can find a solution online or in some book, well and good. But if the process is complicated, then you might have to take some classes in food engineering and food processing to really become an expert.

Sometimes an online course would be sufficient. Sometimes you have to go to university and learn there.

Similar thing applies to biotechnology, engineering, nano technologies, robotics, artificial intelligence, anything.

So, this is how you find a path for your education and decide which courses you should do.

And obviously it goes without saying, this type of learning will not end with university education, you will have to keep learning for the rest of your life.

If you're interested in learning something unique, which is not taught in India, do go outside, learn, specialise and invent.

Education for Invention.

This gives a new importance to engineers. Rather than becoming a salaried employee, even if small portion of our engineers start focusing on becoming inventors and innovators and making great inventions and innovations and building revolutionary products and companies in India; we can create huge wealth, provide lots of jobs and increase our GDP.

My suggestion would be that at the end of your graduation, you should be able to build something that solves some problems.

Our education system divides higher education into different streams. You can either choose to study subjects like physics, math, and engineering, or focus on economics and business studies, or pursue the arts. The idea behind this system was that a student cannot learn everything at once, which is true.

However, the downside of this approach is that it works well if the goal is to produce factory workers. A labour only needs expertise in one specific area. But to become an entrepreneur, apart from having knowledge of science and technology, you also need to understand management, marketing, sales, operations, finance, economics etc.

It's like if you need four strong legs to be a successful entrepreneur but our stream-based education system only strengthens only one leg while leaving the other three weak.

That's why I suggest taking time outside your main course to learn additional subjects like management, marketing, sales, operations, finance, economics, research in science and technologies etc. In new education policy they have introduced some flexibility. But even if they don't teach, you'll have to learn them on your own.

If I ask you, what is the superpower of Tony Stark in Ironman?

He doesn't have an extra-terrestrial superpower.

The superpower of Tony Stark is that he can make Ironman in a cave. He is an innovator.

Being an innovator/inventor is superpower, it can make you rich.

Stock Market

Nowadays we are seeing that among college youth there is a huge trend of learning the stock market and investing money in the stock market. If people are investing and learning to invest, then it is a good thing.

But let us do a little math here.

During student life, students do not have much money, so most students invest only two to five thousand and keep watching the ups and downs of the market throughout the day.

Let us assume that you have made a very good strategy and you get a return of 50-100%, even then you will earn a maximum of two to five thousand only.

We need to understand one thing here that capital is not the only thing that we are investing. We are also investing our time and body.

Because in the above-mentioned case the capital is very small, due to this even after getting a very good percentage return the profit made in absolute terms is only two to five thousand.

On the other hand, if a student buys a course of ₹300-₹500 to learn mobile app development. He invests his time in learning mobile app development and learns it in 6 months to a year, and because of this he gets a salary package of 8-10 lakhs. (We are not talking about business and entrepreneurship right now)

If you calculate the return on those 300-500 rupees invested even with simple interest instead of compound interest, then you will find that the return is 20,000%.
The reason for such a high percentage of return is that these ₹500 were not invested alone, time was also invested along with them, and the time was invested at the right place.

Now if this person invests 10-20 lakhs from his savings in the stock market after getting a job and he gets a profit of only 10-12%, then also in absolute terms he will be earning 1-2 lakhs. Which is much more than the profit of two-five thousand. Therefore, we also need to understand that to get more returns, we should invest our time at the right place.

Summary

✦Many people despite coming from humble backgrounds, specialised in science and technology, engineering and invented or innovated something and sold it to masses eventually became rich.

✦Our education system needs to align itself to produce problem solvers. People who innovate and invent rather than just being labours.

✦At an individual level design your education in a such a way to learn skills that will help you to solve some problems.

✦If you are interested in becoming entrepreneur, along with your main degree, also learn management, marketing and sales, operations, finance etc.

Chapter 8

How Can a Country Get Rich?

In this chapter I will be discussing about five countries, Japan, Israel, USA, China, and India. I do feel for my brothers from global South, that is Africa, South America, Southern Asia. They can also relate themselves with the story of India.

Japan – After the defeat in World War II , atomic attack and despite living near Ring of fire and facing continuous earthquakes and tsunami. Japan has always been the lighthouse for the Asian nations that yes! Wealth can come to us as well. We can be as developed as western countries. Electronics, automobile and all the tech products that Japan has made and manufactured and exported has brought extreme wealth to it.

Israel - what can you possibly make in such a small country?
Tech products.

Despite being surrounded by hostile members, Israel has survived because of its strength in technology on one hand, it helps Israel to defend itself. On other hand. It also becomes its major export. And as we discussed earlier, high end technology brings higher margins and thus, these exports bring a lot of wealth to Israel.

USA – Always been the hub of innovation and technology and capital-intensive industry. If a country that has truly understood the importance of innovation and utilised it to maximum capacity, it's USA. And that's why they are world's largest economy despite having way smaller population than India and China. Technology colleges of USA like MIT, Harvard, Stanford, and the Silicon Valley has been the front runner in cutting edge technology and innovation. The combined market capitalisation of 4 big US tech companies (Google (alphabet), Apple, Amazon, and Meta) is 6 times larger than the combined market cap of all NIFTY 50 companies.

China – The factory of the world. We all know how China became the manufacturing hub. But here I would like to discuss about the part two of China's growth story. I can't put a date when this part started but somebody in China understood that manufacturing for western companies gives you only a smaller share from the big profit this companies make. And thus, by hook or crook, that is by innovation or copying they started their own companies, and they made their own products. Especially in electronics fields, from smartphones to TV, laptop to computers you name it. What we see in form of Xiaomi, Oppo, vivo, Lenovo, Huawei etc, are the byproduct of that brand creation strategy.

In recent years, China has significantly outpaced the United States in the number of patent applications filed. According to the World Intellectual Property Organisation (WIPO), in 2019, China filed approximately 1.4 million patent applications, accounting for 43.4% of the world's total, more than double the number filed by the United States. CSIS

In the realm of artificial intelligence (AI), China's dominance is even more pronounced. Between 2014 and 2023, China filed over 38,000 patents related to generative AI, six times more than the United States, which filed 6,276 in the same period.
(Reuters)

Then there comes the hard-working **India** (Physically).

We are fortunate that we took advantage of computer revolution and today's software are our major exports.

Apart from that, India's other exports are Refined Petroleum, Mineral Fuels, Machinery and Mechanical Appliances, Electrical Machinery, Organic Chemicals, Pharmaceutical Products, Iron and Steel, Rice, wheat, cloth etc.
Many of these exports are tech intensive but we need to make more high-tech products. Then only we will be earning more profit margins and wealth will flow towards India.

If you think in terms of barter, you will realise that we have to give 2800 kgs of wheat for entry level 170 gm iPhone 16. (Considering ₹25 per KG for wheat and 70,000 for iPhone 16.)

Do all the mathematics, how much hard work, time (three months), land, fertiliser, water is required to grow 2800 kgs of wheat. On the other hand, an iPhone, which weights 170g containing some lithium, silicon, aluminium and may be little bit of silver or gold. What's more important is the tech that puts these metals in right way, and the marketing and branding.

I cannot emphasise more on technology, invention, and innovation.

The US invested $2.34 trillion in ventures and startups between
2014-2024. China invested $835 billion. India, in comparison, has only invested about $150 billion.

Here in India, we have been so proud of our Jugad technology. Jugad is enemy of innovation. Jugad is nothing but bad engineering and poor inefficient product designing. Unfortunately, our mainstream media celebrates the jugad but hardly covers any research in any of the universities of India. (Except for The Hindu). Building products is a skill, it has to be learnt by studying engineering. Marley being jugadu will not help.

If India has to grow rich, it will have to research and make products that are world class, durable, and elegant. Products that are competitive at world market. Products for which people are ready to pay higher amounts. Apart from this we also need to focus of global brand building.

New technologies like artificial intelligence, machine learning, nano technologies, bio technologies, 5G, big data, Internet of things, quantum computers, cyber security, etc. provides us opportunities that can help us build great products for the world.

There is no alternative, we will have to sell to the world, especially the richer parts of the world, the western world.

As of 2023, we are net trade deficit country, that means we import more than what we export. So, to become a net exporting country we need to become an innovation hub. We need to educate our younger generation to be innovator.

Lots and Lots of Indian youth spend a lot of time reading the world history in detail. If even the small portion shift to reading and understanding European and other western market and what kind of products and services they need and how can we deliver them. Wealth will start coming to India.

Summary

✦ **Japan, Israel, and USA:** Technology and innovation have been the key drivers of wealth and prosperity in these nations.

✦**China:** China transformed from a manufacturing hub to a global leader in innovation by creating its own tech brands like Xiaomi, Huawei, and Lenovo. With significant investment in R&D, it now leads the world in patent filings, especially in artificial intelligence, outpacing the US in key technological areas.

✦ **India:1. Focus on High-Tech Products**: India needs to move beyond basic exports and develop high-tech, high-margin products, particularly in electronics, AI, and advanced manufacturing, to compete globally.

2.**Invest in Innovation**: India must foster an environment of research and innovation in universities and industries, promoting global competitiveness and encouraging product development that meets international standards.

3.**Global Brand Building**: India should prioritise building globally recognised brands, leveraging its technological expertise and entrepreneurial spirit to capture markets worldwide.

Message

If you like the book, please take a moment to write the review online and also recommend the book to your friends and family.

Thank you

About the Author

Kartik is currently working as a Physics faculty for IIT-JEE and NEET aspirants. He holds a B. Tech. in Electronics and Communication Engineering from NIT Bhopal. Alongside his teaching career, Kartik has a deep interest in technology and global economic trends, constantly exploring new advancements and ideas.

In addition to academics, Kartik is skilled in Devanagari calligraphy, which reflects his creative side and love for traditional art. He enjoys staying active through jogging and cycling and finds solace in reading books.

He currently lives in Surat, where he continues to guide students and pursue his many passions.
You can connect with him on X @kartikrathore25

www.ingramcontent.com/pod-product-compliance
Lightning Source LLC
La Vergne TN
LVHW041104150826
845673LV00007B/1927